FOR THIS WE LEFT EGYPT?

FOR THIS WE LEFT EGYPT?

A PASSOVER HAGGADAH FOR JEWS AND THOSE WHO LOVE THEM

DAVE BARRY

ALAN ZWEIBEL

ADAM MANSBACH

FLATIRON
BOOKS
NEW YORK

FOR THIS WE LEFT EGYPT? Copyright © 2017 by Dave Barry, Alan Zweibel, and Adam Mansbach. All rights reserved. Printed in the United States of America. For information, address Flatiron Books, 175 Fifth Avenue, New York, N.Y. 10010.

www.flatironbooks.com

Illustrations by Ross MacDonald

Designed by Steven Seighman

The Library of Congress Cataloging-in-Publication Data is available upon request.

ISBN 978-1-250-11021-3 (paper over board)
ISBN 978-1-250-11022-0 (e-book)

Our books may be purchased in bulk for promotional, educational, or business use. Please contact your local bookseller or the Macmillan Corporate and Premium Sales Department at 1-800-221-7945, extension 5442, or by e-mail at MacmillanSpecialMarkets@macmillan.com.

First Edition: March 2017

10 9 8 7 6 5 4 3 2 1

This book is dedicated to the Jewish people,
who have a great sense of humor,
we hope.

CONTENTS

FOR THIS WE LEFT EGYPT?

WHAT IS THE HAGGADAH?

By Rabbi Schmooley Weiskopf

The book you hold before you contains the liturgy for the Seder service on this festival of Passover—or, as reform Jews sometimes call it, Chanukah. It tells the story of our people's slavery in Egypt, their release from bondage, and their mass exodus to the Promised Land. It is a much-beloved book, steeped in tradition and replete with prayers and songs of celebration in addition to fun pictures of inedible food and deadly plagues.

Yet what has confounded rabbis and been a source of much theological debate through the centuries is the word *Haggadah* itself. What does it mean?

Some have contended that it does not have a definition, that the word itself defines the text—just as the word *kneecap* has no other meaning than, well, *kneecap*.

In fact, *Haggadah* is not a word, but rather the name of the only former Hebrew slave to drown once the waters of the parted Red Sea unparted. Haggadah crossed safely, but went back to retrieve a sandal that had come off his foot during that hectic rush between the walls of water. As a handful of witnesses overheard and subsequently blabbered to their Old Testament neighbors, the conversation between Haggadah and Moses once they reached the other side was as follows:

"Hey, Moses, do me a favor and keep the Red Sea parted just a few minutes longer? I gotta get my sandal."

"To hell with your sandal, Haggadah! I've got to unpart these waters so the Pharaoh's army drowns. My G-d, it's been hundreds of years since we relaxed."

"So what am I supposed to do?"

"Hop to the Promised Land, Haggadah."

But the portly Haggadah did not pay heed. He waddled back for his beloved sandal (it's been said the pair were a gift from his aged mother shortly before she died of dysentery, leprosy, intestinal worms, plague, scurvy, and exposure), retrieved it, placed it on his foot, turned, and started running in an attempt to rejoin his now liberated brethren. But it was not to be, as the walls of the Red Sea came crashing down upon him—the irony being that about ten minutes later his retrieved sandal washed ashore, where it was reshaped by Moses into a hand puppet to amuse his grandchildren.

And for these reasons, this Haggadah is dedicated to Haggadah.

Happy Passover,
Rabbi Schmooley Weiskopf

P.S.: Then again, I could be wrong. In which case this book is dedicated to my high school track coach, Jim Hart.

A NOTE TO PARENTS

Over the years, countless parents have asked us this question: "Where can I get a good family Haggadah?" Really, it's weird how often this happens to us. We'll be sitting in a public-restroom stall,* and suddenly a head will poke under the door, and it's almost always somebody asking where to get a good family Haggadah. Sometimes these people *aren't even Jewish.* Sometimes they aren't even parents. That's how huge the demand is.

And with good reason. Many young Jewish people today would rather undergo amateur eyeball surgery than sit through a lengthy and boring Seder. With that in mind, we wanted to make this the most entertaining and fun Haggadah ever. We thought about putting Sudoku puzzles in it, or a helicopter-chase scene involving the Pharaoh. We even considered doing the Haggadah in the form of an app, so that younger people could go through the entire Seder without ever looking up from their phones. That's how serious we are about engaging young people.

In the end we went with a more traditional print format. In these pages, you'll find the Seder service accompanied by some Hebrew writing. We frankly don't know what this writing says; for all we know it's a Hebrew repair manual for a 1973 Westinghouse dishwasher. We just felt that there should be some Hebrew in here.

---

* That's right: all three of us in the one stall.

You'll also find discussion questions and activities sprinkled throughout the book. These will make the Seder last longer, so you should ignore them. We also strongly recommend that you appoint somebody as the Seder leader, with the authority to assign reading passages and assess fines for mispronunciations, slow reading, asking too many questions, etc. The Seder leader should have a whistle approved by the Rabbinical Council of America.

Note that this Haggadah follows the traditional Hebrew page-numbering format, which means the first page is located at what would ordinarily be the end of the book, and the last page is located at what would ordinarily be the beginning. It's important for you to remember this, because otherwise you'll tell the Exodus story backward, starting with the Israelites as free people in the Promised Land and ending with them as slaves in Egypt.

But however you tell the story, the important thing is that, as a family, you are carrying on the ancient Jewish tradition of sitting around a table and carrying on a tradition, followed by a soup course. It is up to you, as a Jewish person, to keep this tradition alive by passing it on to your children, so that someday they, too, will purchase this Haggadah, and our children will receive royalties.

We will close with these Hebrew words:

כדי להימנע מקריעה, להרטיב את
אטם הניקוז לפני ההסרה.*

---

* "To avoid tearing, moisten drain gasket before removal."

A NOTE TO GRANDPARENTS

To put it bluntly, you are loathed at the Seder table. Yes, during the other 364 days of the year you are cherished, respected, and tolerated for smelling more like a cedar closet than you once did. You represent happy childhoods to your children, give gifts and tell great stories to their children, and are forgiven for having teeth the same color as Dijon mustard.

But then, in the time it takes to say, "After forty years in the desert, Moses's breath could melt a pyramid," all that unbridled affection unravels because of your insistence that we read every single Hebrew word of an already-long service that stands in the way of partaking in the festive meal. The irony being that these prolonged prayers cannot even be heard above the growling stomachs of the people seated at the table. Hungry adults who have worked all day and battled traffic on their commutes home. Hungry children who've spent the entire day at school and are looking forward to singing "Dayenu" and then stuffing their faces before pillaging the house in search of the afikomen with their cousins. Even hungry pets are eager to forgo the ho-hum blandness of store-bought food in favor of a delicacy like a discarded shank bone.

Is it any wonder that, according to polls conducted by the Federation of Rabbinical Theologians (FART),[*] the Most

---

[*] While the rabbis were well aware that the acronym should have been FORT, a contingent of the least mature of them lobbied in favor of FART because it made them giggle.

Despised People in the Jewish Community List looks like this?

1. Adolf Hitler
2. Osama bin Laden
3. Grandparents at Seders
4. ISIS

Exactly what should be done to stem the mounting tide of disdain and preserve the legacy of this greatest generation? The Federation of Rabbinical Theologians, in conjunction with the recently formed League of United Divine Learned Youth (FARTLOUDLY), maintains that the ball is in the grandparents' court. Your choices are threefold: you can keep your mouths shut and adhere to the wishes of offspring whose turn it is to run their own Seders as they see fit; you can not show up to the Seders until after the meal, when the door is opened and you are dressed as Elijah, which will provide a good laugh for adoring grandchildren, especially if you give them money after their laughs subside; or you can convert to a religion that doesn't eat. The choice is yours.

A NOTE TO EPISCOPALIANS

You have picked up the wrong book.

PREPARING FOR THE SEDER

The first step in preparing your household for the Seder is to get rid of all the *chametz*. We do this to remind ourselves of a time when the Jewish people had a bunch of *chametz* around, and they got rid of it. It's important that we carry on this tradition; the Torah states that the punishment for not removing the *chametz* from your household is *kareth*, which, depending on which rabbinical authority you accept, translates to either "shame" or "death by George Stephanopoulos."

What is *chametz*? It is any substance that contains grain, grain-like ingredients, or grain molecules. This includes bread, pizza, crackers, fortune cookies, soft drinks, vodka, tooth whiteners, certain tropical fish, and all IKEA furniture.

Note that not all breakfast cereals are *chametz*. Froot Loops, for example, are made of compressed medical waste, so they're fine. Jerky is also OK, as is anything named "cheez." But you should get rid of basically everything else in your kitchen, including the appliances. You can make this into a fun activity for the children by telling them that they're going on a "*chametz* hunt," stressing to them that it is going to be very enjoyable. It helps if you drink the vodka first. Dispose of the *chametz* by setting it on fire with a kosher blowtorch, preferably outdoors.

Another fun way to involve the children in the Seder preparations is to take them with you to the supermarket for the tradition of *lacham* (literally, "Fistfight with Other Jews Over the Last Remaining Box of Manischewitz Rocky Road

Macaroons"). The youngsters might also enjoy making up a special song to perform during the Seder. An easy and fun way to do this is to simply take a popular tune and adapt the lyrics to tell the Exodus story, as in this example using the hit song "Hello, Dolly!":

Hello, Dolly
Well, hello, Dolly
Moses led the Jewish people out of slavery in Egypt, Dolly

If you're planning to use props to dramatize elements of the Seder, you should assemble them ahead of time. One fun idea is to give each child a "plague bag" containing items representing the ten plagues. For added excitement, you can represent lice with actual lice, which you can obtain on Craigslist.

Finally, you might want to prepare some kosher snacks and hide them in the bathroom so you can excuse yourself from the table and wolf them down during the two-to-five-hour stretch of the Seder in which there is nothing to eat except matzah. It's OK to do this because, in the words of Rabbi Yehuda "Bud" Epstein (1864–present): "What happens in the bathroom, stays in the bathroom."

Discussion Questions for
"PREPARING FOR THE SEDER"

I'll give you a dollar if you eat every single bit of *chametz* in the house right now. Come on. Do it.

If you had to guess, in what decade would you say a person who thinks of "Hello, Dolly!" as a popular song was born? The 1920s? The 1910s? Earlier?

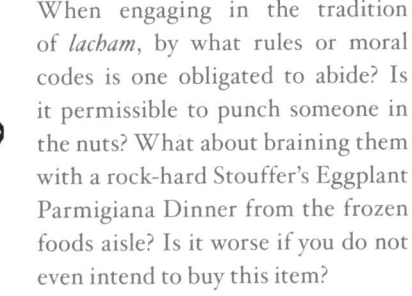

When engaging in the tradition of *lacham*, by what rules or moral codes is one obligated to abide? Is it permissible to punch someone in the nuts? What about braining them with a rock-hard Stouffer's Eggplant Parmigiana Dinner from the frozen foods aisle? Is it worse if you do not even intend to buy this item?

16

Two dollars.

According to some scholars, it is a *mitzvah* to barbecue over the flames of the burning *chametz*. Do you agree or disagree? And why should anybody care what you think?

THE SEDER PLATE

Beitzah
ביצה
(roasted egg)*

Charoset
חרוסת
(chopped apples and nuts)§

Karpas
כרפס
(parsley, celery, potato)†

Maror
מרור
(bitter herb)**

Z'roa
זרוע
(roasted bone)‡

Chazeret
חזרת
(second bitter herb for
Hillel sandwich)††

* Vegans may wish to substitute an "egg" made of Silly Putty, which is guaranteed to taste just as good as any other vegan egg substitute on the market.

† Not to be confused with "carp ass," which is the main ingredient in gefilte fish.

‡ Vegans should note that this bone is just for looking at. Nobody is going to make you eat the bone, so just relax.

§ At least one-third of those attending the Seder must remark that the *charoset* is delicious and their favorite part of the meal, and pledge to make it on some of the other 364 nights of the year. Actually doing so is, of course, prohibited by Jewish law and custom.

   Those with nut allergies should ask themselves how severe their nut allergies really are. If these so-called allergies result in nothing more dire than a mild stomachache and are mostly bandied about in a spirit of "Ooh, look at me, I've got an allergy," then just eat the *charoset*. The same is true of the type of lactose intolerance that can be discreetly neutralized with a pill but is instead exhaustively discussed with the waiter at every family gathering before mysteriously vanishing when dessert is served. We are looking at you, Aunt Phyllis.

** Bitter Herb would be a great nickname. Why aren't there more Jews called Bitter Herb? Especially from the generation that included a lot of people named Herb. Remember those Burger King ads from the 1980s (or, as one of the authors' daughter calls them, chillingly but not inaccurately, "the nineteen hundreds") about searching for and ridiculing Herb, the only guy in America who's never tried a Whopper? Those were stupid.

†† Hillel the Elder—born in Babylon in 110 C.E. and so called because he was elder than everybody else—is one of Judaism's most famed religious leaders, instrumental in the development of the Mishnah and the Talmud and credited with articulating the Golden Rule ("One if by air, two if by sea"). But can we just pause for a second here to reflect on the fact that this dude invented the sandwich EIGHTEEN HUNDRED YEARS before the syphilitic British earl who got all the credit? Why isn't it called a Hillel? Why isn't that other schmuck's version called a Sandwich's Hillel? Granted, putting an edible thing between two other edible things and eating the resulting thing isn't exactly rocket surgery, but still. How many other significant religious leaders have also altered

the course of gastronomic history through invention rather than prohibition? You can bet your sweet tuchus that if Pope Innocent VIII had come up with fondue, every schoolchild would know all about it. But this singular innovation has been swept under the carpet like so much matzah dust. It's a scandal. It really is.

THE SEDER CHECKLIST

- Holiday candles, but not those crappy little Chanukah ones
- Carafe of wine
- Carafe of Long Island Iced Tea (optional)
- Seder Plate (family heirloom; if you do not have a family heirloom Seder plate, just purchase the ugliest plate you can find)
- Cup for Elijah
- Carafe of Long Island Iced Tea for Elijah
- Travel sickness bag for Elijah
- Three matzot, covered
- Thing with which to cover matzot, such as a beautiful embroidered cloth, *Star Wars* pillowcase, or McDonald's napkin
- Matzah of Hope (optional)
- Matzah of Revenge (optional)

- Afikomen bag (can be purchased wherever afikomen bags are sold)
- Pillow(s) for reclining
- Dictionary to answer question of why you can recline, decline, or incline, but you can't just "cline"
- Although there are a few Kleins out there that I wouldn't decline, if you know what I mean
- Heh-heh-heh
- Sorry
- Salt water for dipping
- Additional salt water for skinny-dipping
- Empty chair to symbolize those not free to celebrate
- Empty chair to symbolize those who apparently do not care enough about their families, their culture, or basic human decency to attend
- Empty chair that is just an empty chair
- Chairs for actual people to sit in
- People
- Cup, basin, towel for washing
- That is to say, you wash yourself using these things, not that you wash them
- Though probably they should be clean
- Flowers (optional)
- But they do make it nice
- Empty Jack Daniel's bottle serving as a makeshift vase OR regular vase
- Haggadah for each person
- On second thought, fifteen to seventy Haggadahs (this one) for each person
- *Person* meaning *every person you know*
- Wine cup for each person at Seder
- Except babies

- Not sure about recovering alcoholics; probably OK
- Matzah ball soup made by most-Jewish person in attendance
- If no Jews are in attendance, matzah ball soup from a jar is acceptable
- But it should not be eaten
- Gefilte fish (wild and sustainably caught; avoid farmed gefilte fish if possible)
- Actual meal containing food

WE LIGHT THE CANDLES

Immediately before the blessing over the wine (קידוש) the woman of the house lights candles. Now, according to Jewish law, she should remember not to strike a match to light them as she is accustomed to doing when she lights the Shabbat candles, but should light the match from an existing flame.

As to exactly what the source of that existing flame should be, the rabbis are not in agreement. The revered eighteenth-century biblical scholar Yossel ben Yossel (Yossel Jr.) argued that the existing flame could simply be from a random candle that was lit moments before the lighting of the ceremonial ones. More recently, Rabbi Joachim Levitats, from his cell in a Tel Aviv prison, passionately maintained that "the flames that deliciously flare after any act of arson (הצתה) will more than suffice" before requesting to be placed in solitary confinement so he could touch himself (לאונן) in a manner "too personal to attempt in the general population."

While lighting the candles, three prayers are recited. This number—and the rabbis are in total agreement about this—commemorates the number of sit-ups (כפיפות בטן) that Moses did prior to the slaves' departure from the house of bondage.*

The three prayers are followed by the woman of the house

---

* It is important to note that the scriptures tell us Moses was capable of doing as many as two hundred sit-ups, which he often did as entertainment for the slaves who placed bets on how many he could do after a particularly hard day of slavery. The fact that he only did three before leaving Egypt underscores just how much of a hurry the Israelites were in.

extending both arms, waving them in a gathering motion, and drawing them to her body before covering her eyes with her hands. The significance of the hand-waving gesture is to unite Jews around the world who are lighting candles at that time. As for the covering of the eyes, it symbolizes that the woman does not want to make eye contact with any of those other Jews for fear that some of them may want to borrow money.*

The Talmud tells of Eliahu and his three blind sons, whom he led one by one into a darkened room. First was Blind Son #1, whom he asked, "How would you brighten this room?" Whereupon Blind Son #1 answered, "How the hell would I know? I am blind." So Eliahu smacked him across the face and shouted, "That is not my fault! I begged your mother not to eat the leaves from that foul-smelling plant when she was pregnant with you!"

Eliahu then led Blind Son #2 into the darkened room and asked, "How would you brighten this room?" Whereupon Blind Son #2 answered, "Back off, Dad! I am as blind as one of the bricks we used to make those ugly-ass pyramids!" So Eliahu smacked him across the face and shouted, "I am not to blame! It was your mother who gave you that pet ram who rammed your eyes when you were a toddler!"

Finally, Eliahu led Blind Son #3 into the darkened room and asked, "How would you brighten this room?" Whereupon

---

* For those of you who may be offended that the words *Jews* and *money* appear in the same sentence, feeling that it perpetuates a negative stereotype that we have been trying to shed for centuries, fret not. In fact, we are deeply offended that you would even think that we would stoop so low. And if you would like a detailed explanation describing just how deeply offended we feel right now, please send us $10, and we may or may not tell you.

Blind Son #3 answered, "Please give me two candlesticks and a match that has been lit from an existing flame." And a jubilant Eliahu exclaimed, "Yes! Yes! Here is that match! Now what will you do?" To which Blind Son #3 replied, "I will light these two candles and insert them into your blessed sphincter if you even think about smacking my brothers again. Now lead me out of here and get me some kosher ice cream.'"

---

* True Story

THE SEDER HAS A SPECIAL ORDER

Seder means *order*. Here is the Seder of the Seder. Read it!
That's a Seder!

KADDESH	We say the Kiddush.[*]	קדש
	We drink the first cup of wine.[†]	
UR'CHATZ	We wash our hands.[‡]	ורחץ

---

[*] Yes, this part of the Seder is called Kaddesh, but you say the Kiddush. If you find that confusing, then let's not even talk about the Kiddish, which is a celebratory meal (but not this one) or the Kaddish, which is a prayer of mourning and also a famous poem by Allen Ginsberg. Funny story about Ginsberg: when one of the authors of this book was in high school, he went to see Ginsberg perform and maybe give him some crappy poetry he (the author) had written. He was expecting Ginsberg to have a beard down to his stomach and be shirtless and playing finger cymbals, but this was the early nineties, and instead Ginsberg was wearing a conservative navy suit and was a dead ringer for Irwin Blumer, the superintendent of the school this author was then attending. There was something really creepy and depressing about that. Maybe that was the day this author realized the sixties were really, really over, which probably he should have known already, since he was born in 1976.

[†] First *official* cup of wine, that is. There is no law against "pre-gaming," to borrow a phrase from today's binge-drinking college idiots, with a "Cup Zero" before the Seder begins. Indeed, as Rabbi Eliezer writes, "Getting hammered at a Seder would be uncool, but there is nothing wrong with being lightly toasted from the moment you walk in the door. Particularly if certain members of your extended family are already on the other side of that door, and are eager to share their political views."

[‡] While washing the hands before eating may strike us less as a ritual than an act of basic hygiene, our ancestors were not nearly so prissy. In biblical times, the hands were washed only on three occasions: after

KARPAS	We dip a vegetable in salt water and say the blessing.[*]	כרפס
YACHATZ	We break the middle matzah in half and hide the larger half, the afikomen.[†]	יחץ
MAGGID	We tell the story of Passover.[‡] Four Questions We drink the second cup of wine.	מגיד
RACHTZAH	We wash our hands[§] and say the blessing.	רחצה

---

birthing livestock, on major religious holidays, and before birthing livestock.

[*] Parents may wish to advise younger children to partake heartily of these wilted, salt-water-drenched carrot sticks, as the actual meal is still unfathomably far away. Children may wish to take one bite and then spray partially chewed carrot bits across the table.

[†] In some families, the children hide the matzah, and the adults have to pay a ransom to get it back. The problem with this is that the children may become drunk with power and refuse to return the afikomen unless they are given an Xbox, or possibly a car. In other families, the adults hide the matzah and the children look for it. The problem with this is that inevitably, the adults will either hide it someplace too obvious, resulting in a super lame afikomen hunt, or they will hide it someplace too clever, resulting in the total meltdown of every child under six. To avoid all of these scenarios, you may wish to follow one simple rule: do not have children.

[‡] This is the meat of the Seder. But you can't eat it. It's just the meat in the spiritual sense. Like, you know how you're starving, and you wish you could eat some meat? That is how your heart and soul and brain feel about hearing the nourishing, juicy, succulent story of Passover. But again, no actual eating of any kind is going on here. Drink your wine. There is no more wine after this for a very long time.

[§] You're probably wondering why we're washing our hands, when we just washed our hands, right? There is an excellent reason for this. We just have no idea what it is.

MOTZI	We say the blessings for the "bread"	מוציא
MATZAH	and matzah.*	מצה
MAROR	We dip the bitter herbs in charoset and say the blessing.†	מרור
KORECH	We eat a sandwich of matzah and bitter herbs.‡	כורך
SHULCHAN ORECH	We eat the festival meal.§	שלחן ורך
TZAFUN	We eat the afikomen.**	צפון

---

* In recent years, a new generation of religious scholars has come to question the notion that matzah was invented when the Israelites fled Egypt with bread that had not had time to rise. Instead, they speculate that the Israelites were loath to flee without the early form of cardboard they had recently invented. It worked great for packing their belongings before leaving Egypt, but clearly was never intended to be eaten.

† Though not with our mouths full.

‡ Please note that this is not the Hillel sandwich discussed earlier, but a second, distinct sandwich. So really, the Jewish people have multiple claims to the invention of the sandwich, dating to long before there was even a place called Sandwich, or for that matter a British empire. If you learn nothing else tonight, remember this: everything you thought you knew about sandwiches is a vast anti-Semitic conspiracy.

§ After waiting one billion years to eat, this meal would taste delicious even if it featured balls of ground-up trash fish mixed with matzah dust and slathered with horseradish to mask the taste. Which is lucky, because it does. A little-known fact about gefilte fish: on the 1991 song "What?" by A Tribe Called Quest, rapper Q-Tip declares that "*Kapelka* makes you vomit"—much to the consternation of hip-hop fans, who speculated that *kapelka* was some kind of exotic liquor or perhaps a bad-smelling friend of Q-Tip's. But no: years later, Q-Tip revealed that *kapelka* was actually a severe mispronunciation of *gefilte*. As Rabbi Eliezer writes, "Q-Tip? More like Jew-Tip, am I right?"

** Assuming you can find it; if you can't, the Seder cannot be concluded. This seems like a great premise for a comic film, right? Tell

BARECH	We say the blessing after the meal.	ברך
	We drink the third cup of wine.*	
	Welcome Elijah the Prophet.	
HALLEL	We sing songs of praise.†	הלל
	We drink the fourth cup of wine.	
NIRTZAH	We complete the Seder.‡	נרצה

---

me you couldn't sell that in a room: *Seth Rogen's house is full of obnoxious in-laws, mischievous kids, and weird old friends from out of town, and he just wants the night to end . . . but when the afikomen goes missing, he's forced to endure an endless Seder—endlessly hilarious!* Total four-quadrant movie. Plug in Adam Sandler as the crazy uncle, Andy Samberg as Rogen's putz of a little brother, Kristen Wiig as his type-A wife, maybe Chris Rock as his high-powered boss who's there for some reason—that puppy's doing $200 million domestic, easy. We have got to call our agents.

* After the afikomen, nothing is permitted to pass the lips . . . except for two more cups of wine, to be consumed in quick succession. Why the sudden binge-drinking? Well, the kids are getting really out of hand, for one thing. Letting them eat all that sugar was probably a bad idea.

† While many songs are songs of praise, some may be more appropriate than others. Sir Mix-A-Lot's "Baby Got Back," for example, while one of the finest tributes to the female buttocks in the Western canon, is probably a poor choice. Though, as Rabbi Eliezer writes, "G-d made asses too."

‡ This means it is time to go home. Naturally, this will involve at least forty-five minutes of saying good-bye. What's the old expression? Protestants leave without saying good-bye; Jews say good-bye and never leave. It's so true.

THE FIRST CUP OF WINE

During the course of the Seder, we recite the Kiddush, which is the blessing over the wine, four times. This is because during the Seder, we drink four cups of wine. This is because the Seder is so damn long that the only way to get through it is, as the ancient Hebrews always said, "שיכור כמו גוי ביום המשכורת" (as drunk as a gentile on payday).

The blessing over wine, "Blessed art thou our Lord our G-d, ruler of the universe, who creates the fruit of the vine," praises the Lord, who finished the work of creation on the sixth day, so he rested and drank a lot of wine on the seventh day, which became another topic of lively debate among the rabbis at the historical "Cups of Wine Conclave" in Jerusalem, 1949.

"G-d's name is Art Thou?" asked Rabbi Menachim Fredo.

"What the hell are you talking about?" the other rabbis asked in unison.

(It should be noted that this might very well be the first time that the word *hell* was ever spoken by a group of rabbis in unison.)

"Well, we are blessing Art Thou our Lord our G-d, are we not?"

"We are doing nothing of the sort! If there were a comma after *Art Thou* it might be a different story!" yelled one disgusted rabbi.

"But as it is," they all exclaimed in unison, "you, Rabbi Menachim Fredo, have once again proved that you are not the brightest candle in the menorah on the eighth night of

Chanukah, the Festival of Lights, when all of the candles are lit and displayed proudly in our windows or on the lawns in front of our houses of worship"—which was most definitely the first time a sentence that long was spoken in unison by a group of rabbis.

The rabbis were so depressed from having to waste their time dignifying the staggeringly moronic utterances of Rabbi Menachim Fredo that they voted unanimously to end their conclave and revisit the meanings of cups two through four at a future time with every hope that Fredo by then would have either passed away or converted to another religion.

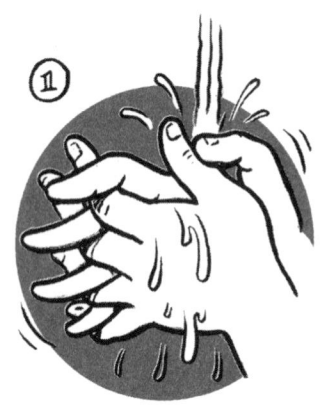

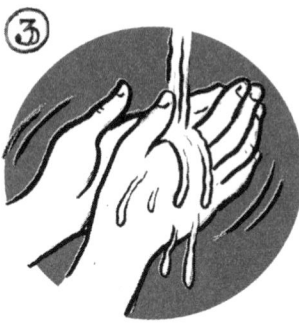

WE WASH OUR HANDS

One of the most oft-asked questions about the Seder is why we wash our hands so oft.[*]

So oft is this question asked that it was actually in the final running to be one of the Four Questions, losing out to "Why do we dip twice?" in the closest vote in Seder history.[†]

Then why *do* we wash our hands so often? The answer is not one of hygiene, as it is in deference to, as we say in modern parlance, delirium. After forty years under the scorching desert sun, the Israelites were totally disoriented. Whenever they asked Moses, "Have we washed our hands?" he invariably replied, "I don't remember. Let's wash them again, just to be on the safe side."[‡]

---

[*] It should be noted that Jews refrain from saying "often" when referring to Passover, and on this note there is virtual unanimity within the rabbinical community, because we were enslaved by the Egyptians for so many centuries that we drop the *en* so as not to remind us of its horror. In fact, there are a few sects that even refrain from using the *en* in the word *century* and spell it *ctury*. And even fewer sects that say *ev* instead of *even*—but those sects, and the rabbis also concur about this, are extremely insane.

[†] For those who wonder why not simply make it Five Questions, it was the consensus among those very same rabbis that the Seder was already long enough and that to have to answer still another question would be futile as the rumbling of hunger pangs of those assembled at the Seder table would drown out that answer anyway.

[‡] According to one account, Rabbi Avram Gamlieal, who said we should wash our hands four times, got into such a heated discussion with Rabbi Yossel "Yo-Yo" Ma, who insisted that anything less than twelve was tantamount to heresy, that the two of them squared off with sharpened shank bones before being separated by the other 2,400 rabbis at the conclave.

WE BREAK THE MIDDLE MATZAH

We break the middle matzah into two pieces, assuming that we can find a piece of matzah in the box that is not already broken. If you cannot find an unbroken piece, you can always whip up a new batch of matzah by following the recipe in the back of this Haggadah,* but keep in mind that this may delay the actual meal by approximately two days.

It is also permissible, with a note from your rabbi, to reconstruct a complete sheet of matzah from the pieces in the box, assuming that you use a glue that is both nontoxic and kosher for Passover.

Wrap and set aside the larger piece. It is now the afikomen, the envy of all the other matzah shards in your household. The afikomen is the "dessert matzah," to be eaten at the end of the meal; the word *afikomen* is actually Greek for *dessert*. If you have any lingering doubts about how bad things were for the Israelites during their bondage and wanderings, the phrase "dessert matzah" ought to clear them right away. The smaller piece of matzah is returned to its place with the other two.

(Uncover the plate of matzah with a flourish, but not so much of a flourish that a matzah shard—this happens more than you might think—flies off the plate and puts somebody's eye out.)

---

* If we remember to write it.

הא לחמא עניא די אכלו אבהתנא בארעא דמצרים. כל דכפין ייתי
וייכל, כל דצריך ייתי ויפסח. השתא הכא, לשנה הבאה בארעא
דישראל. השתא עבדי, לשנה הבאה בני חורין.

Translation: This is the bread of poverty, which our ancestors ate in the land of Egypt.[*] All who are hungry, come and eat.[†] All who are needy, come celebrate Passover with us.[‡] Now we celebrate here. Next year may we be in the land of Israel.[§] Now we are slaves. Next year may we be truly free.

(Fill the wine cups for the second time.)

---

[*] Or, technically, just outside the land of Egypt.

[†] Come and eat some matzah, that is. The actual meal will not be served for some time yet.

[‡] Not that our obligations to the needy should be limited to singing them off-key songs and feeding them brisket once a year. Frankly, that accomplishes very little in terms of eradicating neediness, but it is a nice thought.

[§] Or better yet, Barbados.

THE MATZAH OF HOPE

(Lift a special matzah and set it aside.)

This matzah is set aside as a symbol of hope for those Jews throughout the world who are not free. We used to use a dove, but it kept crapping all over everything. This matzah is for the Jews who are not free to celebrate the Seder. They are not free to express their Jewish identity. Some of them have never even seen *Annie Hall*. They are not free to read Jewish books, to learn of their Jewish past, or to eat Chinese food on Christmas. Their voices have risen in pride and protest, which is ironic since yeast is forbidden during Passover. Tonight we add our voices to theirs. On their behalf, we buy extra copies of this Haggadah.

THE FOUR CHILDREN

We should teach our children about Passover by answering questions that were asked by imaginary children who were made up by adults trying to imagine what children might ask about Passover if they ever stopped looking at their iPhones.

The wise child might ask: "What are the statutes and laws and rules that Adonai our G-d has commanded us?"

We should tell this child the Passover story in excruciating detail. We should read this child the entire book of Exodus, reciting every single statute and law, including all the dietary laws such as "Do not cook a young goat in its mother's milk." When we are finally done answering the wise child's question, everybody will be very tired, and the brisket—which started out hot and juicy and was to be the main course of the Seder meal—will be as moist and tender as a UPS truck tire. And the wise child, if he or she is truly wise, will never ask this question again.

The wicked child might ask, "So it's okay to cook an older goat in its mother's milk?"

Not really! That was just a little Passover humor.* But seriously:

The wicked child might ask: "What does the Passover service mean to you?"

---

* As Rabbi Eliezer said, "You can't spell 'Haggadah' without 'Ha.'")

The wicked child is basically saying that he or she does not consider himself or herself part of the service. We respond to this child by giving him or her a very fatty slice of brisket.

The simple child might ask: "What is this?"

To this child, we respond, "With a strong hand, Adonai our G-d brought us out of Egypt." And the simple child might then say, "No, I meant, what is this thing crawling on the Seder plate?" This is an opportunity to have a group discussion about the importance of thoroughly washing the shank bone.

Finally, we have the child who does not know enough to ask a question.

We explain to this child that the secret is to take a declarative sentence, then simply reverse the order of subject and verb.

I am chopped liver.

What am I, chopped liver?

Discussion Questions for
"THE FOUR CHILDREN"

How would *you* explain Passover to each of the four children? Do you think you could do a better job than this Haggadah?

There is a thin line between confidence and arrogance. How might thinking you are better than we are cross or not cross that line?

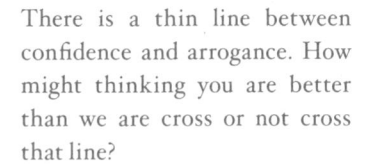
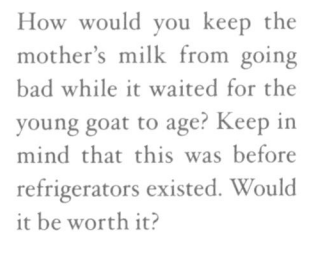

How would you keep the mother's milk from going bad while it waited for the young goat to age? Keep in mind that this was before refrigerators existed. Would it be worth it?

Should brisket be made with beer or wine? What about carrots? Caramelized onions? Can we all agree that prunes in brisket are disgusting?

Vito "The G-dfather" Corleone had four children:[*] Sonny, Fredo, Michael, and Connie. At Corleone family Seders, who do you think asked each of the four questions, and why?

Have you ever met a child who cannot ask a question? Wouldn't it be great if such a child existed, especially on long car trips?

---

[*] Tom Hagen, an orphan whom Sonny brought home and who once told Sonny, "I'm as much a son to him [Vito] as you or Mike," does not count. Though it's certainly revealing that he didn't say, "you, Mike, or Fredo." Clearly, Tom considered himself more of a Corleone than Fredo. This seems likely to be accurate; as Rabbi Eliezer has written, "Fredo got dropped on his head as an infant."

What do we mean when we say that Adonai our G-d had a "strong hand"? Is this a poker reference? Write an alternate telling of the book of Exodus in which Adonai our G-d challenges the Egyptian sun god, Ra, and the Egyptian hippopotamus goddess of childbirth, Taweret, to a game of cards to determine the future of the Jewish people.

Would Adonai our G-d bluff? Would he have to? Who would bring the chips to such a poker game? If Adonai our G-d "forgot" to ante up, would the others have the guts to call him on it?

THE PASSOVER STORY

The Passover story begins thousands of years ago in the land of Egypt, which is located in the Middle East, unfortunately. Egypt was ruled by a man called the Pharaoh, who was very powerful. Like one time he said, "I want a pyramid," and although it took many years, a group of Egyptian workers *actually built him a pyramid*. When the Pharaoh saw it, he was very surprised, because what he actually wanted was some soup, which in ancient Egyptian sounds very similar to the word for *pyramid*. So everybody had a good laugh, and then the Pharaoh had the workers executed, because that's how embarrassed he was.

So anyway, around this time,[*] a nice Jewish boy named Joseph arrived in Egypt, and he came to be an advisor to the Pharaoh because he had a degree in management. He advised the Pharaoh to build storehouses to store the grain, which the Pharaoh thought was a tremendous idea, because up to that point he had been storing the grain in the bathroom, and it was disgusting. The Pharaoh was so pleased that he invited Joseph to stay in Egypt and bring his relatives to hang out also. They became known as the Israelites, and they multiplied and prospered in various fields, although generally not team sports.

Years passed, and eventually the Pharaoh died. (He was buried in the pyramid, which by then the Egyptians jokingly

---

[*] 4:45 P.M.

referred to as "the Big Stone Soup.") A new Pharaoh took over, and he turned out to be a real schmuck. He was afraid that the Israelites would become too powerful, so he made them into slaves, which for the Jewish people was a very difficult time requiring its own subheading in **boldfaced type**.

SLAVERY

Slavery totally sucked. The Pharaoh made the Israelites work from sunrise to sunset with no days off, not even Labor Day. The Israelites were forced to do hard work, such as hewing stones, which, as you would know if you ever hewed a stone, is no picnic. But the Israelites continued to multiply, so Pharaoh Schmuck decreed that every male baby born to an Israelite woman had to be cast into the River Nile, where they ran a risk of, at minimum, getting a cramp, particularly if they were cast too soon after eating a heavy meal.

There was an Israelite couple named Amram and Yocheved who had a male baby, but they didn't want him to be cast into the Nile. So instead, they hid him for three months. Then they put him into a basket, and, to make absolutely sure he was safe and would not be cast into the Nile, they put the basket . . .

OK, they put the basket into the Nile. But it was OK because they used an ancient Egyptian car seat. Their daughter, Miriam, hid in the reeds and watched to see what happened next, which you will find out in the next paragraph.

As it happened, at that moment, the Pharaoh's beautiful daughter was bathing in the Nile, which she preferred because the Pharaoh's bathroom still smelled faintly of grain. She noticed this baby floating past in a basket, and she said, "I shall keep this baby, as apparently it does not belong to anybody!" Yes, she was beautiful, but dumber than a brick.

Miriam stepped out from behind the reeds and offered to raise the baby and have her mom (who of course was Yocheved, the baby's real mother) be the nurse. The Pharaoh's daughter was like, "Sure!" So, bottom line, this woman went to take a bath and came home with a baby *and* two new domestic employees. We can only imagine what she would have done with a credit card. She decided to name the baby Moses, which was an ancient Egyptian word meaning either *drawn from water* or *soup*.

MOSES GROWS UP

As the subheading above suggests, Moses grew up. He lived a life of luxury as the prince of Egypt in the Pharaoh's palace, but he was upset about the treatment of the Israelites. One day, he saw an Egyptian beating a slave, so Moses killed him (the Egyptian) and had to flee from Egypt, making his escape by riding off on a speedy young sheep, which is where we get the expression "on the lamb."

Moses went to the land of Midian, where he became a professional shepherd, which was a living. One day, he was shepherding on Mount Horeb when he saw a bush that was on fire and speaking in a voice that sounded kind of like

Morgan Freeman's. This turned out to be G-d, who told Moses that he was going to rescue the Israelites from slavery and take them to a land flowing with milk and honey. This raised several questions in Moses's mind, such as:

1. Were the milk and honey flowing separately, or mixed together?
2. Were they flowing right on the ground?
3. Wouldn't that attract insects?

But this did not seem like a good time to interrupt.

G-d told Moses that he should go back to Egypt and tell the Pharaoh to let the Israelites go or G-d would bring plagues down upon the Egyptians, and Moses said, "OK," because when a divine, all-powerful, flaming shrubbery tells you to do something, you do it.

Discussion Questions for
"THE PASSOVER STORY"

The Pharaoh who hired Joseph and welcomed the Israelites to Egypt seems like he was pretty chill, but his son turned out to be a major putz. This kind of thing seems to happen a lot. Look at Han Solo and Kylo Ren, for example. Or Martin and Charlie Sheen. And there are also putzes whose kids turn out cool, like our friend Caitlin, whose dad is a real putz. What were we talking about again?

Would you store grain in a bathroom? Why or why not?

According to scripture, Moses had a speech impediment. Some scholars believe that Adonai chose a leader with a handicap to prove that he does not require perfection. Others argue that all the other Israelites had even worse speech impediments. And still others hold that Moses just had a slight lisp you could barely notice and it was no big deal. Which group of scholars do you think is the most fun at parties?

THE TEN PLAGUES

Moses asked the Pharaoh to free the Israelites, but the Pharaoh refused because he was a schmuck. So G-d brought ten plagues upon Egypt, and each time, the Pharaoh got scared and promised to free the Israelites, but he did not, because in addition to being a schmuck he had the IQ of a glazed doughnut. It was only after the tenth and scariest plague that it finally dawned on his tiny Pharaoh brain that unless he wanted G-d to turn the entire Egyptian population into sea urchins or something, he'd better let the Israelites go.

We fill our cups with a *meh* wine that we do not mind spilling to remember how happy we were when this happened. But we are not totally happy, because we are Jewish, and thus we can never be truly happy except when the Knicks win the title. Also we feel a little bad for the Egyptians, because it's not like they had a democracy and said, "Hey, let's elect a moron to be the Pharaoh!" So instead of drinking all the wine or even a nice martini* right now, we dip our fingers into our cups and spatter wine droplets all over a perfectly good tablecloth, which will have to be dry-cleaned—but go ahead, it's fine—as we say the names of the plagues:

---

* G-d, that would improve the Seder.

Blood
Humidity
Frogs
Nervousness
Lice
Constipation Like You
   Would Not Believe

Locusts
Jerry Lewis
Boils
Gluten

Discussion Questions for
"THE TEN PLAGUES"

If you could visit ten different forms of living hell on an entire country to punish a leader the people hadn't even elected, which country would you choose? Would you feel like a big man afterward?

Is Manischewitz even a *meh* wine? Could it, perhaps, be considered a plague?

Form two "teams," one made up of all the children, and the other made up of all the adults. Act out the conversation between Moses and the Pharaoh, with the children asking the same question over and over and over again, and the adults saying, "*No, no, no, no, no, no, no, no, no, no, FINE.*" It feels just like real life, doesn't it?

CROSSING THE RED SEA

Shortly after letting the Israelites leave Egypt, the Pharaoh realized he had made a terrible mistake. Sure, killer angels had just slaughtered a large percentage of his people's children, and the streets were a disgusting stew of blood, frogs, and locusts, and it was hailing and dark, and everybody had lice and boils, and Jerry Lewis *would not shut up*. But on the other hand, the Pharaoh had just lost his free labor force, to say nothing of what the Israelites' departure was going to do to the Egyptian entertainment industry. Also, the Pharaoh was a huge fan of gefilte fish, which his Egyptian chefs couldn't seem to get right no matter how hard he had them flogged.

So the Pharaoh sent his army to bring the Israelites back. His soldiers caught up with them on the banks of the Sea of Reeds, where the Israelites were discussing the fact that a sea of reeds seemed to be blocking their escape route.

When they saw the Egyptian army, the Israelites were afraid and cried out, "Oh crap! Boy, are we royally screwed now! No pun intended!" But they were wrong, for at that moment, Adonai told Moses to lift his rod. Moses was briefly uncomfortable with this command, but then he remembered that he was carrying a walking stick. He raised it, and a strong east wind parted the waters of the sea, leaving space for the Israelites to cross over dry land and also pick up an array of interesting seashells that would have otherwise been inaccessible.

The Egyptian army, none of whom apparently had been paying the slightest attention to anything happening in Egypt over the previous couple of weeks, decided it would be a good idea to follow them.

Moses lifted his rod again, and the waters rushed back and covered the Egyptian soldiers, along with their horses and chariots. We forgot to mention that they had horses and chariots. That was why it was so easy for them to catch up to the Israelites. Anyhoo, they all died a horrible death. Then Moses's sister, Miriam, led the women in joyous dance and song, thanking Adonai for saving their lives. They tried to get Moses to dance, but he declined despite the ballroom dancing lessons he had taken when he was a prince.

"You should save your strength," Moses advised. "We still have to walk to the land of Canaan, and it is at least ninety minutes away." He was correct, in the sense that it took longer.

THE STORY OF PASSOVER:
DELETED SCENES

In a standard Haggadah, the story of Passover ends with the crossing of the Sea of Reeds. This is because the authors of most Haggadahs have not promised their publishers that they would deliver a manuscript of no fewer than ninety-six pages.

WANDERING IN THE DESERT AND/OR WILDERNESS

After crossing the Sea of Reeds, the Hebrews spent forty years wandering in the desert, also referred to as the wilderness. Initially, this was because Moses (like many typical male prophets) refused to ask for directions to the land of Canaan. But later, other factors emerged: when twelve Hebrew spies did manage to sneak into the Desert of Paran, on the edge of the Promised Land, they discovered that while the soil was fertile, the land was inhabited by giants. Yup, that's right. Giants. Though it is also possible that the twelve spies were all really short, or that they happened to reach the Desert of Paran on Stilt Day.

In any case, the people were afraid of the giants, and many wanted to return to Egypt. This was super lame, and Moses told them that they were not worthy to enter the Promised Land. Instead, they would wander in the wilderness for forty years, until the generation that had refused to enter died and instead their children would inherit the Promised Land. Weirdly, the issue of giants never came up again.

The Israelites did not greet this new plan with enthusiasm, as it pretty much called for several decades of just hanging around, waiting to kick the bucket. The supply of matzah had been gone for months at this point, and the Israelites were sick of eating sand for breakfast, lunch, and dinner. Moses knew he had to do something to boost morale, or these people were going to lose their minds. Luckily, Adonai our G-d knew just what to do. As is so often the case with our people, the solution came in the form of food.

MANNA FROM HEAVEN

For the next forty years, the Israelites were nourished by a substance that fell from heaven. It was fine and flaky, like divine dandruff, and it arrived with the dew every night. The Israelites gathered it before the morning sun caused it to melt, and they pounded it into cakes, which were then baked. Stored manna went bad overnight, but on the Sabbath a double portion of manna fell, and this manna did not spoil, so that no gathering of manna had to be done on the Day of Rest.

Scientists and historians have speculated—this is true—that manna might have been anything from plant lice to a resin created by aphids to a kosher species of locust to psychedelic *Psilocybe cubensis* mushrooms, but those jerks are missing the point, which is that manna came from heaven and the Israelites ate nothing else for forty years, not even ranch dressing.

Classical rabbinical literature holds that as a supernatural food, manna produced no waste products, and thus the Israelites did not defecate during their wanderings. Classical rabbinical literature further holds that this lack of defecation caused the Israelites to complain, and that they were worried about potential bowel problems. As Rabbi Eliezer observes, "Not much has changed since then, in terms of Jews and a preoccupation with pooping or not pooping."

THE TEN COMMANDMENTS

Moses and the Israelites came to a mountain called Mount Sinai, which was also known as Horeb.* There they made camp, which was hard because Jews are not into camping. Our idea of roughing it is a hotel where the breakfast buffet does not have an omelet station.

Anyway, on the third day of camping, a giant cloud descended on the mountain, making the sound of a trumpet,† so the Israelites gathered around to find out what the hell was going on. Then G-d spoke from inside the cloud. At least he *said* he was G-d; there was no way to tell for sure because of the cloud. Whoever was in there told the Israelites there was going to be a covenant featuring Ten Commandments. This made the Israelites nervous, because it sounded strict. Up to that point, they had been operating under the Ten Suggested Guidelines, which included "Thou shalt try to keep the noise down" and "No peeing on the campfire."

So Moses went up into the cloud to get the Ten Commandments. He was gone for forty days and forty nights,‡ which works out to four days per commandment. It was like getting a covenant from the Department of Motor Vehicles. He was gone so long that the Israelites became very upset and—we

---

* Sometimes it was also called Doug.

† Specifically, "Hello, Dolly!"

‡ As opposed to forty days and thirty-nine nights, which would have been a little cheaper.

have all done this in times of stress—made a Golden Calf and worshiped it.

Finally, Moses came down with the Ten Commandments, which were written on two stone tablets because G-d had used a large font. When he saw the Golden Calf, he became ticked off and threw the tablets on the ground, breaking them. Fortunately, they were still under warranty, and G-d wrote out another set of commandments, although he changed some of the wording to eliminate the phrases "a well-regulated militia" and "Honey, while you're out can you get me some stool softener?" These are the laws that we still obey today, except in a literal sense. Moses placed the tablets in the Lost Ark, which was stored for safekeeping in a large government warehouse.

THE GOLDEN CALF

Among the more controversial stories pertaining to the exodus from Egypt is the one about the Golden Calf. So contentious have these discussions gotten that on at least four occasions (though by some accounts the number is closer to eleven hundred), the Jewish National Guard had to be called in to break up the squabbling rabbis.[*]

First, let's start with what the rabbis do agree upon—that Moses, the recently freed slaves' liberator, took leave of them and went up Mount Sinai to receive the Ten Commandments and that because he was up there for forty days and forty nights, the Israelites started getting antsy. "Hey, what's he doing up there?" they said in unison. "How long does it take to get a few measly commandments?"

So the Israelites, fearing that Moses would not return, began losing faith and demanded that Moses's older brother, Aaron, make them a new god. So Aaron gathered up their golden earrings and ornaments and constructed an idol for them to pray to and exalt for bringing them out of the land of Egypt.

It is at this juncture that the controversy as to exactly what the icon that Aaron constructed looked like begins.

"Golden Calf," claimed Rabbi Leslie "Cool Jew" Lewis, whose yarmulke sits atop an unusually wavy head of hair. "It was a Golden Coif."

---

[*] Squabbling Rabbis would be a good name for a band.

"Utter nonsense," said Rabbi Chaim Tuchman, whose obsession with physical fitness is manifested in a bumper sticker that reads *Keep the Flex in Genuflects*. It was his contention that thanks to the exceedingly long trek across the desert, the slaves' legs became highly muscular and thus Aaron cobbled an idol of his own right calf.

"Wrong!" exclaimed Rabbi Bernard "Redundant" Bernard, whose assertion that the calf was of the offspring-of-a-cow variety is the widely held belief.

Whatever the graven image was, when Moses came down from the mountain and saw it, he got angry and threw the two stone tablets upon which the Ten Commandments were chiseled at the calf, thus setting it on fire.

"I leave you in charge and this is what you do?" yelled Moses.

"What did I do?" asked Aaron, blushing like older biblical brothers tended to do when they were playing dumb.

"You built an idol, which pretty much negates what Judaism is all about!"

"You mad at me, Mo?"

"It doesn't matter if *I'm* mad. *He's* the one you have to worry about," said Moses, pointing back toward the top of the mountain. "He's the one who parted the Red Sea. My guess is that it would be a lot easier for him to part you."

Moses gave one last look at the smashed stone tablets, the smoldering ashes of the Golden Calf, and the hungover Israelites sleeping on top of each other in various states of undress after a debauched night of blasphemous partying, then shook his head and headed back up the mountain to ask G-d for a new set of commandments.

Aaron, feeling guilty and ashamed, made a final plea to his younger brother. "Moses, can you get me off the hook? For old times' sake?"

Still another fact that all the rabbis agree upon is that this line of dialogue was infinitely more effective when Abe ViG-da's character said it in *The G-dfather*.

Discussion Questions for
"THE GOLDEN CALF"

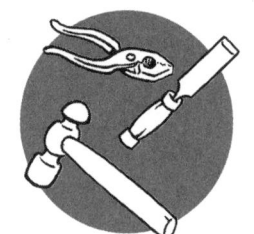

Where the hell did the Israelites get enough gold for a Golden Calf? What tools did they use to make it, considering they left Egypt so fast they couldn't wait for the bread to rise?

Was that line actually more effective in *The G-dfather*, considering that it's basically the last thing Tessio says before Tom Hagen has him killed?

Why not a Golden Brisket?

THE PROMISED LAND

Because the Israelites had ticked G-d off, they did not get to go directly to the Promised Land. Instead, they wandered in the desert for forty years. Which is a lot of wandering, when you think about it.

Let's say for the sake of argument that a standard Israelite wanders five hundred steps per day, with an average distance of two feet per step. That works out to a thousand feet per day. So for more than forty years—even if they didn't wander at all on Shabbat, major Jewish holidays, Elie Wiesel's birthday, and so on—the Israelites would wander about twelve million feet, which is more than two thousand miles. This means that, starting in Egypt, the Israelites could easily, with minimal exertion, have wandered to Norway.

And yet, somehow, after forty years, they were *still in the desert*. This suggests they were not wandering in anything close to a straight line. Many Jewish scholars have pondered the reason for this, but perhaps the best explanation was offered by Rabbi Moscowitz,* who said, "They must have been hitting the sauce pretty hard."

By this point, Moses was over one hundred years old, and most of the other original Israelites were dead. The rest had been born in the desert and after all the wandering were getting pretty cranky. "Are we there yet?" they constantly asked Moses. But Moses was not discouraged, because by

---

* This would be Rabbi Dirk Moscowitz, brother of Rabbi Shane Moscowitz.

this point he had basically the same hearing ability as a crowbar.

So long story short, they *finally* reached the Promised Land, but it turned out that Moses was not allowed to enter because of a problem with his passport.

"Don't worry about me," he told the Israelites. "I'll just go up on Mount Nebo and die. Alone. After all I've done for you. It's fine. Really."

So the rest of the Israelites entered the Promised Land, which turned out, G-d had not mentioned this, to be already occupied by a number of tribes, including the Canaanites, Hittites, Amorites, Perizzites, Hivites, Kardashians, Mohicans, Kiwanis, and a small but enthusiastic roving band of Mormons. Also, instead of milk or honey, there were rocks and venomous scorpions the size of Yorkshire terriers. But other than that, it was everything the Israelites had hoped for, and for the next three thousand years, they lived there in peace and harmony except for getting nearly wiped out on pretty much a monthly basis. And that is why we are grateful.

THE PASSOVER SYMBOLS

Rabbi McMullen said that when we tell the story of the Exodus, we should explain the meaning of the three most important symbols, or else everybody will wonder what the hell they are doing on the table where the edible food should be.

PESACH

(Point to the shank bone. If this is a vegetarian Seder, point to the beet. If this is a vegan Seder, point to the beet and announce that it is unacceptable because it could be tainted with worm doody.)

The shank bone comes from a lamb. Let's call her Sally. Sally did not suffer. One minute she was munching on some hay or whatever lambs eat, not noticing the kosher butcher approaching with a kosher mallet, and the next minute, *bang*, she was Passover chow. Try not to think about it. We probably shouldn't even have brought Sally up.

Anyhoo, Sally's bone reminds us that our ancestors were way more badass than we are. They didn't buy their lamb bone from the pre-sacrificed meat section of the supermarket. They used to personally sacrifice an actual live lamb. Or, if they were vegetarian Jews, they would sacrifice a live beet.

This bone (or beet) reminds us that during the tenth plague, G-d passed over the homes of the Israelites and spared the male children of the Israelites. We frankly don't know *why* the bone (or beet) reminds us of that. It just does, similar to the way the song "Hanky Panky" by Tommy James and the Shondells reminds us of throwing up Singapore Slings in the parking lot of the Willow Inn in Armonk, New York.

MATZAH

We eat matzah because it reminds us that our ancestors had to skedaddle out of Egypt in a big hurry, and they wanted to carry with them a food that was not only very lightweight but could also be used as both a weapon and a building material.

MAROR

We eat the maror to remind ourselves that we never, ever again, as a people, want to be in a position where we have to eat freaking maror.

WE SAY THE BLESSING FOR MAROR

(Give everyone a piece of maror and some *charoset.*)

We dip the maror into *charoset* to recall that our ancestors were able to withstand the bitterness of slavery because it was sweetened by the hope of freedom. The bitterness of persecution because of the sweetness of love. The bitterness of exile because of the sweetness of family. The bitterness of family because of the sweetness of bourbon. The bitterness of ill health because of the sweetness of complaining. The bitterness of acid reflux because of the sweetness of Pepto-Bismol. The bitterness of Joe Piscopo because of the sweetness of Eddie Murphy.

בָּרוּךְ אַתָּה יי אֱלֹהֵינוּ מֶלֶךְ הָעוֹלָם, אֲשֶׁר קִדְּשָׁנוּ בְּמִצְוֹתָיו וְצִוָּנוּ עַל אֲכִילַת מָרוֹר.

Baruch Atah Adonai Eloheinu melech ha'olam asher kid'shanu b'mitzvotav v'tzivanu al achilat maror.

We praise you, Adonai our G-d, ruler of the universe, who makes us holy by your mitzvot and commands us to eat maror.

(Eat the maror and *charoset.*)

WE EAT A SANDWICH OF MATZAH AND MAROR

(Distribute pieces of maror and the bottom matzah.)

Back in the days of yore,* Rabbi Hillel was famous for many things—his wisdom, inventing both the Golden Rule and the Five-Second Rule, and possessing the ability to belch the entire Hebrew alphabet (including the vowels). But perhaps more than anything, he was notorious for spending Passover walking around the Temple in Jerusalem eating delicious sandwiches made of Pesach (the lamb offering), matzah, and maror. Hillel was renowned as a just and generous man, but if you asked him for a bite of that Passover sandwich, he would kick you in the face. Nowadays, we do not bring sacrifices to the Temple,† so our sandwich is made only with matzah and maror. This is known as the Great Outrage.

---

* So called because they contained unprecedented levels of Yore.

† Instead, we sacrifice to afford tickets to the High Holidays.

DAYENU

Possibly the most joyous song sung at the Seder is "Dayenu." Not only is it a favorite among children, as this catchy tune inspires rhythmic clapping, but it is generally followed by the festive meal, which is reason enough to start applauding.

In addition, "Dayenu" exemplifies the rush the slaves were in when leaving Egypt, because this six-letter word translates into the fifty-seven-letter phrase "That alone would have been sufficient, for that alone we are grateful."

"On the face of it, that may not seem like a lot. But when one considers that the word is sung four times in each stanza, and that the song has fifteen stanzas, and that there are two Seders every Passover, and that the average life expectancy is now 78.7 years, if you add up the time that all of those 'Dayenus' save, you can go on safari for a month," said Rabbi Mpho Pretorius of South Africa. "Or explore the fjords," said Rabbi Sven Jepsen of Norway. "Or be our guests on a cruise down the Nile as a small token of how badly we feel about what we did to you guys," said Rabbi Maaravi Abubakar of Egypt.

The song's first four stanzas are about freeing us from slavery.

If he brought us out of Egypt . . . Dayenu
If he had executed justice upon the Egyptians . . . Dayenu
If he had slain their firstborn . . . Dayenu
If he had boiled their firstborn and made a delicious soup . . .
Dayenu

The next five stanzas are about the miracles.

If he had split the Red Sea for us . . . Dayenu
If he had delivered us to dry land . . . Dayenu
If he had drowned our oppressors . . . Dayenu
If he had minced our oppressors and served them with paella . . .
*   Dayenu*
If he took the paella and molded it into statues of Abbott and
*   Costello . . . Dayenu*

And the final five stanzas are about being with G-d.

If he had given us Shabbat . . . Dayenu
If he had led us to Mount Sinai . . . Dayenu
If he had given us the Torah . . . Dayenu
If he had charged us for the Torah . . . Dayenu
If he had put photos of the Beatles and Lady Gaga's cell number
*   in the Torah . . . Dayenu*

WE EAT THE FESTIVE MEAL!!!!!!!!!!

!!!!!!!!!!!!!!!!!!!!!!!!!!!!

!!!!!!!!!!!!!!!!!!!!!!!!!!!!

THE THIRD CUP

(Lift wine cups, or, if this is a Cinco de Mayo–themed Seder, tequila bottles.)

Baruch Atah Adonai Eloheinu melech ha'olam borei p'ri hagafen.

Translation: We praise you, Adonai our G-d, ruler of the universe, commander of the cosmos, capo di tutti capi, Lord of the Rings, queen of the prom who creates the fruit of the vine and all the varietals thereof, including (but not limited to) your merlots, your cabernet sauvignons, your zinfandels, and, for the dessert course, your sauternes; and who, more importantly, created fermentation, without which we would never get through the entire Seder without stabbing ourselves in the eyeball with a fork.

(Drink the wine.)

WAITING FOR ELIJAH

At the conclusion of the delicious meal, after grace has been recited, a fifth Kiddush cup of wine is poured and placed at the center of the table. The front door to the home is then opened, and another prayer is recited as everyone waits for the prophet Elijah to enter and take a sip from his cup.*

The opening of the door is a reminder that G-d protected the Jews from the plague that slew all the Egyptian firstborn during the night of the first Seder. Therefore, opening the door expresses our trust in G-d's protection.†

It is also of note that Elijah is the one who visits the circumcision ceremony of every Jewish male child and testifies that Jews are scrupulous regarding the practice of circumcision. This is significant because according to the Talmud, males were only able to eat from the paschal lamb if they were circumcised. So, in effect, Elijah comes to the Seder to "testify" that all males present are circumcised.‡

---

* This is not to be confused with Seders at Samuel Beckett's home where a fifth of Irish whiskey was filled, the door was opened, and Vladimir and Estragon waited for G-dot to enter.

† This is not to be confused with Seders in certain uptown neighborhoods where the front doors are opened and hoodlums (whose names could very well be Elijah) enter and, after drinking from the Kiddush cup, steal the Kiddush cup along with all of the Seder-goers' jewelry and their hosts' TV sets at gunpoint.

‡ To our knowledge this is the first time circumcision has been referred to four times in one paragraph in *any* Haggadah. Celebrate with another cup of wine!

This welcoming of Elijah is the second half of the Seder. While the first half is the commemoration of the exodus from Egypt, this second is an allusion to the forthcoming arrival of the messiah that will be announced by Elijah.[*]

---

[*] This is not to be confused with Elijah Wood's announcement, as Frodo Baggins in *Lord of the Rings*, that he would carry the Ring of Power to Mount Doom and there cast it into the flames from whence it was forged. Though certainly the two statements are related.

Discussion Questions for
"WAITING FOR ELIJAH"

What would happen if Elijah drank from the cup? Not in terms of the messiah but on a physiological level. Would the wine pass through him, ghost-style, and end up on the rug? How much wine would it take to make Elijah drunk? Is that even possible? Presumably, if the messiah is coming, Elijah has got to put in an appearance at every single Seder in the world, which—aside from being a logistical nightmare—means a lot of wine. Kind of like Santa Claus with the milk and cookies, though obviously there are fewer of us (Jews) than there are of them (cookies). Make a collage that answers these questions.

How come the Angel of Death needed lamb's blood to know which houses the Israelites lived in? You'd think that would be the kind of thing the Angel of Death would just know, right? Also, doesn't it seem weird that the slaves would live in houses next to and indistinguishable from the people enslaving them? Make a papier-mâché sculpture that answers these questions.

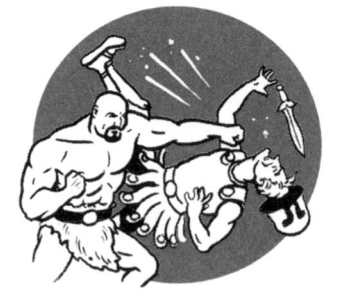

According to scripture, Elijah wore a hairy coat with a leather belt, called down fire from heaven to scorch his enemies, presided over the raising of the dead, put an end to the worship of the Canaanite god Baal, and left earth in a chariot of fire pulled by horses of fire. Why has there never been a major motion picture or video game about Elijah? Is that anti-Semitic? Should Bruce Willis play Elijah, or can you think of someone better? Definitely not Dwayne "The Rock" Johnson. What about Jeff Goldblum? That would be kind of interesting. He hasn't done much lately, has he? Make a friendship bracelet that answers these questions.

"ECHAD MI YODEA"

Numbers are important in Judaism, as any of the accountants or Kabbalah weirdos at your Seder can attest. This traditional Seder song helps us "count with meaning" and would be great to sing with the kids if they hadn't all gone to watch a video in the bedroom two hours ago.

Who knows one? I know one
One is our G-d who is in heaven and earth
Or rather on earth, since that is the proper preposition
To modify earth
Though these rules are rather subjective
And only G-d knows why you are on Manhattan or in Brooklyn
Especially with the rents these days
You might as well move to Queens
Am I right?

Who knows two? I know two
Two is the number of fingers in the peace sign
Which we display in photographs
To remind us of the fallacy of war
Or to make air quotes
If we are douche bags

Who knows three? I know three
Three is the holy trinity
Of delicatessen fish options

Whitefish, lox, and sable
Although an argument for kippers
Could also be made

Who knows .328? I know .328
.328 is Wade Boggs's lifetime batting average
I have no idea why I know that
But I will take it to my grave

Who knows four? I know four
Four are the acceptable types of bagels:
sesame, poppy, onion, and everything
Get out of here with your blueberry bagel
Your asiago cheese bagel
Your Saint-John's-wort bagel
And all the rest of these
fugazy bagels

Who knows five? I know five
Five are the books of the Torah
And the boroughs of New York City
But none among us
Has the wisdom to say
Which book is Staten Island

Who knows six? I know six
Six are the books of the Mishnah
Which is the most Jewish book ever
Even more Jewish than Portnoy's Complaint
Because it is basically one long argument

Who knows seven? I know seven
Seven are the days of the week
For it was Adonai our G-d who gave us
The weekend to chill and created
Labor unions to enforce it

Who knows eight? I know eight
Eight is the punch line to that counting joke
That doesn't really make any sense because
Who sevens a tree? What does that even mean?

Who knows nine? I know nine
Nine are the months of pregnancy
Which is how we make more Jews
Because going door to door is for schmucks

Who knows ten? I know ten
Ten are the commandments
Which Adonai our G-d gave Moses
At a rate of one commandment every four days
Because chiseling stone is difficult
And presumably they also took breaks
To just hang out

Who knows eleven? I know eleven
But I'll be damned if
I tell you

Who knows twelve? I know twelve
Twelve are the tribes of Israel

Whom we honor by being
Unable to name more than like two

Who knows thirteen? I know thirteen
Thirteen is bar or bat mitzvah
When a Jewish child becomes an adult
Which maybe made sense when
The average lifespan was twenty-nine but
Seriously, have you spoken to a
Thirteen-year-old lately?

"CHAD GADYA"

This is a fun traditional Passover song that takes about four hours to sing correctly.

One little goat, one little goat
That my father bought for two zuzim
The retail price is three zuzim
My father gets a discount because he buys a lot of goats
Along came a cat and ate the goat

Which sounds ridiculous until you realize that this song is an allegory about the history of Israel, with the cat symbolizing Assyria.

Along came a dog, symbolizing Babylonia, which bit the cat
Guess where it bit the cat?
On its ASS(yria)!

Ha-ha! We are having some fun with this traditional allegorical song!

Then along came a stick

Apparently, it was a walking stick
Stop it! We are killing ourselves with this wordplay!
Anyway, the stick symbolized Persia by hitting the dog

Along came a fire, aka Greece, and burned the stick
Along came water in the form of Rome and put out the fire
Along came an ox symbolizing the Saracens

Which, according to Wikipedia, is either an early Arab tribe
Or an English professional rugby team
Whoever they were, they drank the water

Along came a butcher, symbolizing the Crusaders, and killed the ox
Along came the Angel of Death, symbolizing the Ottomans—
    which sounds like a horde of lethal footstools, right?—and
    killed the butcher
Along came the Holy One, symbolizing the Holy One, and slew
    the Angel of Death
And a partridge in a pear tree

WE COMPLETE THE SEDER

THE FOURTH CUP

(Lift cups, bongs, syringes, etc.)

Baruch Atah Adonai Eloheinu melech ha'olam borei p'ri hagafen.

We praise you, Adonai our G-d, ruler of the universe, CEO of the world, supreme commander of all creation, and elite quarterback of the heavens, and we thank you for providing us with the fermented fruits of your vines in liquid form that has gotten us through the Seder for another year unless we are one of those Jewish families that does this whole thing again tomorrow night, you forbid.

But at least for now our Seder is over. We want to take this opportunity, since this is a new paragraph, to thank you once again, Adonai our G-d, for being such a supreme being. We look forward to celebrating Pesach for many years to come, until we have to gum the matzah for fifteen minutes before we can swallow it, which we will do because it reminds us of something, although by that point we probably will not remember what.

(Point to the shank bone again.)

Somebody please put that thing in the garbage.

THE FIFTH CUP

Some families drink a fifth cup of wine in gratitude for the state of Israel and also, depending on the playoff situation, for the Knicks.

THE SIXTH THROUGH SEVENTEENTH CUPS

There is no point in letting perfectly good wine go to waste.

ABOUT THE AUTHORS

Dave Barry is a Pulitzer Prize–winning humor writer whose columns and essays have appeared in hundreds of newspapers over the past thirty-five years. He has also written a number of *New York Times* bestselling humor books, most recently *Live Right and Find Happiness (Although Beer Is Much Faster)*. He is not Jewish, but many of his friends are.

An original *Saturday Night Live* writer, **Alan Zweibel** has won numerous Emmy and Writers Guild of America awards for his work in television, which also includes *It's Garry Shandling's Show* (which he co-created), *Late Show with David Letterman,* and *Curb Your Enthusiasm*. He collaborated with Billy Crystal on the Tony Award–winning play *700 Sundays*, and he won the Thurber Prize for his novel *The Other Shulman*. Unlike Dave Barry, he has no Jewish friends.

Adam Mansbach is the #1 *New York Times* bestselling author of *Go the F*** to Sleep* and *You Have to F****** Eat*, as well as the California Book Award–winning novel *The End of the Jews*, a dozen other books, and the movie *Barry*. His work, which has been translated into more than forty languages, has appeared in *The New Yorker, The New York Times Book Review, Esquire,* and *The Believer* and on National Public Radio's *All Things Considered* and *This American Life*. Dave Barry and Alan Zweibel are his only friends.